I0118820

James Greene

Manual of the First Presbyterian Church of Indianapolis

James Greene

Manual of the First Presbyterian Church of Indianapolis

ISBN/EAN: 9783337292997

Printed in Europe, USA, Canada, Australia, Japan

Cover: Foto ©Lupo / pixelio.de

More available books at **www.hansebooks.com**

WITHDRAWN FROM MBNEH

MANUAL

OF THE

First Presbyterian Church

OF

INDIANAPOLIS.

TOGETHER WITH

A HISTORY OF THE SAME,

FROM ITS

ORGANIZATION IN JULY, 1823, TO NOVEMBER 12, 1876,

BY

REV. JAMES GREENE,

OF THE PRESBYTERY OF INDIANAPOLIS.

INDIANAPOLIS:
JOHN G. DOUGHTY, BOOK AND JOB PRINTER.
1878.

HISTORICAL DISCOURSE.

Behold! I have graven thee upon the palms of my hands: thy walls are continually before me.—*Isaiah* xlix : 16.

THE history of this church has its origin at a period only about two years later than the organization of the town itself. The Legislature, at its session in January, 1820, appointed a Commission of ten persons to select a site for the capital of the State. Only five accepted the trust. These gentlemen, after examining various localities, finally settled upon two, one of which they agreed should be their final choice. These were the mouth of Fall Creek, and the Bluff's of White River. After thorough examination of both, and abundant discussion of the advantages afforded by each, they proceeded to determine the question by vote, when the present locality was chosen by a majority of one. The Legislature, at its session in January, 1821, confirmed the choice of the commissioners, and at the suggestion of the late Judge Sullivan, of Madison, one of the committee appointed to draw up the Bill of Confirmation, conferred upon the infant capital its euphonious and appropriate name.

As soon as this important measure was adopted,

population began to gather in, and amongst the earliest settlers were a few Presbyterian families. The first sermon from a Presbyterian Minister was preached by Rev. Ludwell G. Gaines, a Missionary from Ohio, on the 21st of August, 1821. The service was in the open air, under the shade of a spreading walnut, near the southwest corner of Washington and Mississippi streets. The youthful chorister of that service, not long since passed away in the person of the venerable and esteemed Col. Samuel D. Maxwell.

Mr. Gaines appears to have spent but one Sabbath with the infant settlement, and the next ministerial visitor was Rev. David C. Proctor, who came in May, 1822, as a Missionary of the Connecticut Missionary Society. He spent one week here, preaching several times, and so far to general acceptance, that measures were taken to secure his services for one-half the time, from the first of October following. During this interval, Rev. Isaac Reed, a Missionary under the Presbyterian Board of Missions, visited the locality and preached on several occasions. He was a man of very moderate abilities, but of commendable zeal and industry in the Master's work. He was much addicted to publishing narratives of his tours and other autobiographical matter, and left two or three small volumes of such literature.

On the first of October, Mr. Proctor returned in pursuance of the engagement made with him in the previous May, which, however, was modified so as to secure three-fourths of his time, in consideration of which, he was to receive $400, or, it was discreetly provided, "so much of it as could be collected." At the expiration of the year thus stipulated for, the congregation did not desire to retain Mr. Proctor's services longer, and he left. Subsequently he married in Virginia, and soon after removed to Kentucky, and spent the remainder of his life in that State. He died January 17th, 1865.

In his ministry with this infant church, Mr. Proctor gave a promise of usefulness that was hardly redeemed by his riper years. He was well furnished by education for his work, and at the beginning of his career, manifested enthusiasm in it. Becoming possessed of a considerable estate, however, by his marriage, the care and increase of it divided his time more than evenly with the work of the ministry. His preaching lost its vitality and force. It does not appear that he was ever settled as a pastor, though usually preaching to one or more small churches in his vicinity. He was distant and frigid in his manners, and formal in his speech: thus failing to add by personal influence to the effect of his ministrations, and falling below the measure of usefulness that might justly have been expected of him.

During Mr. Proctor's ministry, efforts were made to secure a house of worship. A subscription was set on foot and $1,200 pledged to the object. A frame building, fifty-four feet by thirty-four was erected on part of the spot now covered by the "Talbott Block," on North Pennsylvania street. The building was begun

in May, (1823,) and so far completed as to permit of
public worship being held in it on the first Sabbath of
the following July. The building committee consisted
of Dr. Isaac Coe, James Blake and Daniel Yandes—
the last still living, a hale and active octogenarian.
The committee discharged their trust vigorously, but
found that the amount subscribed would be deficient
several hundred dollars. But the wit of pioneers be-
comes sharpened by exigencies, and the committee was
equal to this emergency. Dr. Coe and Mr. Blake carried forward the work to completion, the carpenters
agreeing to take their orders on Mr. Nicholas McCarty,
the only merchant in the village, for goods, and Mr.
McCarty generously agreeing to honor such orders and
wait the convenience of the committee for payment.
The inconvenience growing out of the scarcity of
money was thus overcome, and a neat and convenient
house of worship, suited to the day and to the people,
was erected and completed. The cost of the building
and the ground was $1,600.

Hitherto mention has been made of the material
fabric only. The policy of these sturdy builders of
"the church in the wilderness," was different from
that most generally adopted. It is common first to
organize the body of believers into a church, and then
to erect for it, with such expedition as may be, the
material and local habitation. The founders of this
church adopted the opposite course, and built a house
for God, before there was a church to occupy it. They
were not, however, any less diligent in the completion

than in the inception of their plan. On Saturday,
July 5th, 1823, a church organization was effected,
eight persons presenting letters of dismission from
other churches, and seven being received on examina
tion, making the total of the original membership
fifteen. Rev. Mr. Proctor was assisted on this occasion
by Rev. Isaac Reed, already mentioned, and by Rev.
William Martin, who arrived here on that day, being
on a journey. The organization was effected in the
celebrated Cabinet Shop of Caleb Scudder, where, also,
preaching was held during the summer. Dr. Coe and
Mr. Scudder were elected elders, and on the following day, being Sabbath, July 6th, the sacrament
of the Lord's Supper was administered in the new
church. On July 7th, the church, by vote, requested
to be taken under the care of the Presbytery of Louisville, at that time the nearest and most convenient
one. During the same month a weekly prayer meeting was begun, and thus the infant church, (its founders having been for a year past active workers in the
Union Sabbath School,) was fully equipped and furnished for work in the Master's cause.

After Mr. Proctor's departure at the close of his
first year of service, an invitation was addressed to
Rev. William Martin, who had assisted at the organization of the church, to return, but the letter failed to
reach him until six months after its date, and the
church, meanwhile, had sought a minister elsewhere.
Attention had been drawn to Rev. George Bush, a
licentiate of the Presbytery of New York, then at

Morristown, New Jersey. He was invited to visit the church, and in compliance therewith, arrived here on the 9th of July, 1824, bearing the commission of the General Assembly as a Missionary.

Mr. Bush entered immediately upon his labors, which met with such acceptance that in September following, he was unanimously called to the pastoral charge of the church, at a salary of $400. The church had now been transferred to the Presbytery of Salem, and Mr. Bush was ordained and installed by a committee of that body, on March 5th, 1825, the service being held in the Court House, as the new church was at that time receiving some finishing touches. Mr. Bush attended the General Assembly of that year as a commissioner, and on his return in July, brought his wife with him, to whom he had been married in his absence from his charge.

In November, 1826, the Session was enlarged by the election to the eldership of Messrs. Ebenezer Sharpe, John G. Brown and John Johnston.

The years 1827 and '28 were a season of severe trial. Although Mr. Bush at his ordination, had given full assent to the Form of Government of the Presbyterian Church, it is not easy to see how he could have done so sincerely. It came to light that he had previously expressed doubts as to the scripture warrant for that system, and soon after his settlement, frequently and boldly denounced it from the pulpit as contrary to the law of Christ. This gave the Session much concern. They remonstrated with the pastor, and being unwilling to proceed to extremities in view of his general acceptableness and ability, they besought him to withhold the expression of his views in public; but to this he would not consent. In April, 1827, he was requested by the Home Missionary Society to visit the East, for the purpose of exhibiting the needs of the West, and arousing interest in its behalf. Before leaving he addressed an elaborate communication to the Session, in which he set forth his views of the scripture idea of church government. Dr. Coe, in his record of the fact, says, "the plan thus embodied was not like any system on earth." During Mr. Bush's absence, which continued until October, a very elaborate correspondence on the matter in controversy was maintained between the Session and himself, in which the polemic talent of Dr. Coe, and the classic pen of Ebenezer Sharpe, did valiant service for the truth.

Finally, after Mr. Bush's return, the church applied to the Presbytery of Wabash, to which it had been transferred, for a dissolution of the pastoral relation. The Presbytery assembled and dissolved the relation. Mr. Bush carried the case by complaint to the Synod. The Synod ratified the act of the Presbytery. Mr. Bush angrily and defiantly avowed his determination not to leave the field; and for nearly a year, still claiming to be pastor of this church, he preached in the Court House, being sustained by a subscription of non-professors, and members of unevangelical bodies. His supporters finally wearied of this burden, and in March, 1829, he left for the East and returned no more.

He never sought another pastoral charge. Several
years were spent in the Hebrew professorship of the
University of New York, and in the service of the
American Bible Society, for both which positions his
great attainments in oriental literature eminently
fitted him. But finally he gave the strongest possible
proof of the wisdom of the first Session of this church,
in obtaining a severance from him, by adopting the
faith of Swedenborgianism. He held to the vagaries
of that system until his death, which occurred in 1859,
at the age of 63 years.

With fine talents and large attainments, Mr. Bush
lacked that balance of mind which insures steadfast-
ness of purpose; and by the death of his wife, which
occurred at an early period in her married life, he was
deprived of an influence that was eminently conserva-
tive and restraining, in the quarter where he most
needed it.

In October, 1828, nearly a year before Mr Bush's
withdrawal, Rev. John R. Moreland, of the Presbytery
of West Lexington, Kentucky, accepted a Call to the
vacant pastorate, though no record is found of the date
of his installation. He had enjoyed no early oppor-
tunities of education, not even learning to read until
he was eighteen years of age. Several years of his
early manhood were spent as a flat-boatman on western rivers. Of course he did not enter the ministry
until comparatively late in life. His preaching, naturally, was not characterized by polish of diction or the
graces of oratory, but did abound in a rugged and

pointed eloquence that was not destitute of impressive-
ness and effect. He also by laborious and conscientious
study, overcame in a great degree, the disadvantage
of lack of early training, and beside much general
information, acquired a very respectable knowledge of
the original languages of the scriptures.

The church, while Mr. Bush was preaching in the
Court House, had held no services except by occasional
supplies, and the membership had, to some extent, become scattered and disheartened. Mr. Moreland gathered the elements together again, and by the blessing
of God upon his energetic labors in and out of the pulpit, the church was revived and strengthened. During
the first eighteen months of his ministry, sixty persons
were added to the church, making the total membership exactly one hundred. His valuable labors were
terminated by death, after a pastorate of less than
three years, on the 13th of October, 1832. It was during his ministry that the venerable James Blake, now
gone to his rest, and James M. Ray, co-workers in the
vineyard for so many years, united with the church by
a public profession of faith.

Rev. William A. Holliday served the church as
Stated Supply for two years from February, 1833
During most of the remainder of his life he was a
worshipper in this congregation. He died December
16th, 1866, and by his liberal benefactions to the cause
of christian education, by the memory of his upright
life, and Christ-like spirit. "he, being dead, yet speak-
eth."

In September, 1834, Rev. James W. McKennan, of Western Pennsylvania, visited the church by invitation, and his labors proving acceptable and useful, he was installed as pastor on the 16th of June, 1835. When he became a subject of renewing grace, he was pursuing the study of law, but from a conviction of duty, abandoned further preparation for that profession, and devoted himself to the ministry. He is described as a man of sincere and eminent piety, of respectable attainments, not brilliant in his pulpit efforts, but sound, instructive and edifying. His connection with the church was terminated at his own request, for what cause is not recorded, in April, 1839, though at the earnest request of the church, he continued to serve as Stated Supply until the following October, when he accepted a call to the church of Circleville, Ohio. Subsequently, he was settled over several other churches, and for several years filled a chair in Washington College, Pennsylvania. His laborious and useful life was terminated at the age of 57, on the 19th of July, 1861.

During Mr. McKennan's ministry here of about five years, one hundred and forty were added to the church, among whom were some who are still bearing the burden and heat of the day in this same vineyard; and yet, when Mr. McKennan resigned his charge, the entire membership numbered but one hundred and thirty. Three causes help to account for this fact. Death had transferred many to the church above; a number of others had removed beyond the bounds of

this church, and during this ministry a number had
withdrawn to form the first Episcopal church organized
in the town. Their preferences, and the membership
of some, had previously been with that body; but as
long as no church of their first choice existed here,
they wisely gave their aid and influence to that organization where they could be most comfortable and useful. And also during the same year, (1837,) that great
division of the Presbyterian Church occurred, causing
two branches, known until the happy re-union in 1869,
as the Old and the New School. This church, like
many others, felt the effect of that concussion, and
fifteen members, (eleven males and four females,) withdrew and formed the organization now known as the
Second Presbyterian Church, the original one from
that time taking the designation of the First.

It is gratifying to state that while many similar di-
visions of churches at that time resulted in bickerings,
strife and even litigation, nothing of the kind occurred
here. The seceding party asked for a just and equitable
division of the church property, and appointed two of
their number, Messrs. Daniel Yandes and Samuel Mer-
rill, to represent them in the negotiation. Dr. Isaac
Coe and Mr. James M. Ray, were appointed a similar
committee on the part of this church. A basis of
action was readily agreed upon, and the transaction
completed to the satisfaction of both parties, in a fra-
ternal and christian manner. How good and how
pleasant it is to be able to say, that from that day to
this, no root of bitterness, no envy or uncharitableness

has sprung up between the venerable mother and the loving daughter, now herself developed into healthful and active maturity. In locality, it has happened that they have always been, and are still likely long to be, near neighbors. In faith and zeal and efficient working for Christ, may they always be found, side by side, striving together against the common Enemy, for the salvation of souls, and the glory of God.

From October 1839, the time of Mr. McKennan's departure, until the beginning of the following year, the church had no regular supply. In January, 1840, Rev. Samuel Fulton, a licentiate, was engaged for the period of three months. At the expiration of that time he was unanimously called to the pastoral charge, but being apprehensive that his health would not endure this climate, he desired that the Call should not be prosecuted.

In seeking their next pastor, the church made application to the Professors of Princeton Theological Seminary, and asked to be recommended to a suitable man among the students about to graduate. They were put in correspondence with Rev. Phineas D. Gurley, a licentiate of the Presbytery of North River, New York, who was accordingly invited to supply the church for the period of six months. Mr. Gurley accepted the invitation, and arrived on the ground in October, 1840. When only two months of the term had expired, he received a unanimous Call to the pastoral care of the church. It was accepted, and the installation took place on December 15th, 1840. This relation continued until November, 1849, being a few days short of nine years, when it was dissolved at Mr. Gurley's request, he having accepted a Call to the First Church of Dayton, Ohio.

It is a noteworthy fact that the fourth pastorate was, by a little over six months, the longest that has existed in this church to this day, that of Dr. Nixon, the seventh, being next. The result of Dr. Gurley's ministry, (that degree being subsequently conferred upon him,) were alike strengthening to the church, and creditable to himself. Seasons of revival were repeatedly enjoyed during his ministry, some of the fruits of which still continue among us.

Dr. Gurley was ranked among the able men of his day in our church, though probably very few have had less reason to complain of being rated below their worth. In his preaching he was clear and practical; in his utterances solemn and deliberate; and not being a specially ready speaker, he was accustomed to write his sermons in full, and deliver them from the manuscript. His voice, naturally deep and mellow, was improved by diligent musical cultivation, and lent its charm to the general effect. In his several pastoral charges he enjoyed a more than average degree of popularity. Beside the merit of his preaching, his social manners were affable, though always dignified; his piety was warm and earnest, and his heart responsive to every call of sympathy. These traits made him welcome both to the pulpits of his brethren and the firesides of his people. He was called away in the

zenith of his power, while filling his third pastoral
charge, that of the F Street Church, in the city of
Washington. He died at his home in that city, on the
30th of September, 1868, at the age of 51.

In the first year of Dr. Gurley's ministry, it became
evident that the frame church building on Pennsylvania street was "too strait" for the congregation, and
measures were adopted looking to the erection of a
larger house, and in a more eligible locality. The
building and lot were transferred to Dr. Isaac Coe, for
$250 in cash, and lot 14, in block 45, which was
adopted as the site of the new house, being the North-
east corner of Market and Circle Streets, now occupied
by the Printing House of the Indianapolis Journal
Company. A plan for the proposed church was pre-
pared by Mr. John Elder, and a Building Committee
appointed, consisting of Messrs. Coe, Sheets, Blake,
Blythe and Elder. The house was to be of brick.
The corner-stone was laid with due ceremony, on the
7th day of October, 1841, and the building was sol-
emnly dedicated to the worship and service of Al-
mighty God, on the 6th day of May, 1843. The
sermon was preached by the pastor, a portion of which,
with the prayer of dedication, is preserved among the
Records of the Congregation.

The edifice of which we have been speaking, and
of the final disposal of which, in 1866, it will be appropriate to speak in another place, is hallowed in the
memory of many of you as the theatre of four succes-
sive and able pastorates, in each of which the ministry

ot the word was made effective, not only by the ordinary, but also by extraordinary manifestations of the power of God's Spirit, in the renewing of his people, and the conversion of sinners.

At Dr. Gurley's resignation, the Session consisted of the following elders: Dr. Isaac Coe, Caleb Scudder, John Johnston, James Blake, James M. Ray and Samuel Bigger, the last of whom was elected while Governor of the State

Rev. Charles S. Mills, Principal of a Female Seminary in the town, supplied the pulpit with acceptance, from November, 1849, until September of the following year.

The Session having become weakened by the removal of several of its members, Messrs. Charles Axtell, (who subsequently entered the ministry,) Horatio C. Newcomb and Thomas H. Sharpe, were, on February 27th, 1850, elected elders, Mr. Axtell, however, having been previously ordained to the office in another congregation.

In September, 1851, while the church was still destitute of a pastor, twenty-one members, including elders Scudder, Blake and Newcomb, requested letters of dismission, for the purpose of organizing another church. The request was granted, and the organization soon after effected by a Committee of the Presbytery of Muncie. Twenty additional members withdrew soon after to aid the new organization. This was the origin of the Third Presbyterian Church of Indianapolis, which has now just completed the 25th

year of its existence. The many tokens of the Divine
favor it has enjoyed, and the prosperity and usefulness
it has attained show conclusively that it was founded
in accordance with the will of God; and in a probable
new locality, an enlarged sphere of active usefulness
seems to be opening before it.

In the fall of the same year, (1851,) a Call to the
pastoral, charge was addressed to Rev. John A. Mc-
Clung, of the Presbytery of Ebenezer, Kentucky, which
was accepted, and the installation effected on the last
day of the year. Dr. McClung's ministry of nearly
four years, (he received the degree of Doctor of Divin-
ity after leaving this charge,) resulted in a large increase to the membership of the church, and uniformly
drew to it the strangers in the city, and very frequently the prominent and resident members of the
bar, connected with other congregations, or with none.
The Session was also enlarged during his ministry by
the election of the late William Sheets, and Thomas
MacIntire, in 1854; the latter having been ordained to
the office in Columbus, Ohio.

Dr. McClung exists in the memory of many of you
as a character marked by strong and notable traits.
The present occasion admits of nothing more than
the merest outline of his remarkable and eventful life.
He was converted at the age of 16, while absent from
home at school, and from a deep conviction of duty,
soon resolved on devoting his life to the service of
God in the ministry. Accordingly, he entered the

Theological Seminary at Princeton, at the age of 18: but ill health, growing out of injudicious medical treatment during a severe illness while at school, compelled him to withdraw after an attendance of eighteen months. He pursued his studies however in private, as his health permitted, and in 1828, was licensed by the Presbytery of Ebenezer. He at once took high rank as a preacher, and the strongest hopes were entertained of his usefulness and success. But these hopes were soon blighted. In his extensive reading he included some infidel works, and finding himself unable to answer some of Gibbon's arguments, and not taking into account his own youthfulness, and comparatively small mental discipline, he imbibed doubts of the genuineness and authenticity of the Scriptures. With his characteristic candor, he laid the matter before the Presbytery, and asked leave to surrender his license. The Presbytery could not refuse the request, but treated the case with all possible gentleness, especially under the advice of a venerable member, who declared his conviction that Mr. McClung would yet see his error, and return. He now directed his attention to the study of law, and in due time entered upon the practice of that profession, in the city of Maysville, Kentucky, where he pursued it for fifteen years. During that period he attained a prominent rank among the ablest advocates in the State, and also rendered valuable service in the Legislature, filling the Speaker's chair during four several terms.

B

But during this period of mental activity and growing reputation, his mind was not at ease as to the claims of christianity upon him. He had never been an infidel in the broad sense. He had never wholly ceased enquiry as to the divine origin of christianity, and finding nothing in the works of infidels conclusive against it, he was through all the years of his legal practice, the prey of a harrowing anxiety and doubt. But he never lost his respect for religion, nor failed to treat and speak of it with reverence. Finally, in 1848, Rev. Dr. Grundy, pastor of the church in Maysville, while preaching upon one of the points that had formerly disturbed Mr. McClung's faith, was led to draw the bow at a venture, and send an arrow that wounded this strong man between the joints of the harness. Not so, however, as to bring him at once a willing captive to the feet of Jesus, but to induce him once more to review the grounds upon which he had, long years before, surrendered his faith in the scriptures. He felt that the habits of investigation he had acquired at the bar, with his enlarged resources and increased mental discipline, would enable him to pursue such an investigation, at least with more satisfaction to himself than he had done in earlier life. He also became acquainted for the first time with a work by an eminent Scotch jurist, in which Gibbon's arguments were answered, and his mis-quotations and sophisms exposed. Under these circumstances he addressed himself again to the great problem before him with all the power of his rapid, comprehensive and disciplined mind. The

labors of his profession compelled him to pursue these
exhausting studies, for the most part, in the hours
when nature demanded repose. The "midnight oil"
illumined them, and not seldom burned on until ex-
tinguished by the dawn. The struggle was long and
the conflict terrible. But the result was the inevitable
one, when a candid and earnest seeker after truth ap-
plies himself in humility and sincerity, to learn the
mind of God from his revealed will. His skepticism
vanished; a light beyond the brightness of the sun
shone round about him; the scales fell from his eyes,
and his prostrated soul put forth the agonizing cry,
" Lord what wilt thou have me to do?" With the return of his early faith, his early convictions of duty
also returned, although it was a pecuniary sacrifice of
no small extent to relinquish the income his profession
was yielding. But he was not one to count the cost,
where convictions of duty were concerned. He applied to Presbytery for license to preach the gospel.
He was licensed accordingly, and returned to the work
of the ministry. with more than his old-time zeal and
earnestness, first as a temporary supply of one of the
churches of the city of Louisville. His ministrations
took strong hold of the public mind at once, and at
the close of that temporary engagement, he accepted
the Call of this church.

To those of you who were privileged to enjoy his
ministry, the characteristics of it are freshly borne in
mind. You remember his plain, direct, colloquial
style, never obscuring the simplicity of the gospel in the

vanity of a showy rhetoric, but always presenting *the thought*, with clearness and force. As he had himself passed through a terrible spiritual conflict, his discourses, to a great degree, took their complexion from it. They were, perhaps imperceptibly on his part, largely addressed to the skeptical mind, and often embodied an affluence of scripture knowledge of massive logic, and fervent appeal that could not fail to shake the citadel of unbelief. He also delighted in the discovery of correlations between the Old Testament and the New, and some of his expositions of that kind were striking and attractive in the extreme. In the winter of 1854–5, he devoted the Sabbath evening services for several weeks to a course of lectures on the prophecy of Daniel, which filled the old church to repletion, and elicited profound interest in the community.

But failing health compelled him in 1855, to resign his charge, to which, after long hesitation, the church gave a reluctant assent. A winter in the South, before resigning his charge, failed to benefit him, and on withdrawing from this church, he resolved to try the cold dry and bracing air of Minnesota. That climate so far restored him that he felt able after a respite of a year or two, to resume the ministry, and was unanimously invited to the pastoral charge of the church of Maysville, Kentucky, and was installed in June, 1857. His labors were largely blessed in an increase both of the membership and the spirituality of the church; and the singular compliment was frequently paid him by the ministers of other denominations, of dispensing with their own Sabbath evening services, that they and their congregations might enjoy the privilege of hearing him.

But after an earnest and faithful ministry of two years there, his health again became precarious, and a period of rest and recreation indispensible. He accordingly left home on the 3d of August, 1859, and on Friday the 5th, arrived at Tonawanda, a village on the Niagara River, about nine miles above the Falls, intending to spend the Sabbath there. But learning there was no Presbyterian church in that village, he started on Saturday afternoon, the 6th, to walk to the town of Niagara, as is supposed, with a view of spending the Sabbath there. Being an expert swimmer, and much addicted to bathing in cold water, the clear broad stream beside his path, held out an invitation he could not resist. He was a stranger in that locality, and no friendly voice was at hand to warn him that those still waters flowed with invincible power, as if gathering strength for their final plunge. He entered the stream. What followed then—whether some physical debility paralyzed him, or whether after a vigorous and manly struggle with the mighty current he was finally overcome, or what thoughts coursed through his brain when a sense of his awful situation flashed upon him— can never be known. This only is known. He was swept on and over that fearful cataract, and his bruised and larcerated body was, some days after, rescued from the whirling eddies miles below, and committed

to the grave by stranger hands. Not there to rest,
however; loving friends of his congregation traced out
his obscure grave, and bore his honored remains to
their final rest, amid the scenes of his youth, and of
the labors of his latest years.

Dr. McClung's connection with this church ceased in
October, 1855, and it was without a pastor, though not
without almost regular supplies for the pulpit, until
December, 1856. In the meantime, Calls had been
given to two ministers; one to Rev. Alexander R.
Thompson, of Staten Island, New York, who intimated
his acceptance, but felt constrained to withdraw it on
account of the destruction by fire of his library, manu-
scripts and most of his personal property. The other
to Rev. Robert S. Hitchcock, of Baltimore, who filled
the pulpit several Sabbaths, but declined the Call.

In November, 1856, Rev. (now Dr.) Thomas M. Cunningham, of Carrondolet, Missouri, a minister of the
Associate Reformed Presbyterian Church, having resolved to change his relation, visited us by invitation,
and spent several Sabbaths. On the 12th of December,
a unanimous Call was made for his pastoral services,
which, after some delay, owing to other Calls made to
him, he accepted, and was installed on the 7th of May,
1857. He was in the vigor of his manhood, fervid and
impassioned in his style of preaching, and at times
profoundly impressive. His ministry was owned of
God, and large accessions were made to the membership, especially from among the young, and for the first
time the need of a larger house of worship began to

be perceived and discussed. Dr. Cunningham withdrew in May, 1860, after a service of three years, having accepted a call to the South Church of Chicago. Subsequently, he was settled for several years over the Alexander Church of Philadelphia, where his labors were also greatly blest. He is now the useful and efficient pastor of the Central Church of San Francisco.

During Dr. Cunningham's pastorate, (in 1859,) it was deemed expedient to establish a German Presbyterian Church. By the aid of a legacy left for benevolent purposes by Mr. Benjamin J. Blythe, a former deacon of the church, a lot was purchased on South New Jersey Street, and a neat brick building erected. The legacy of Mr. Blythe was supplemented by donations from this church, and the enterprise was set on foot even to the installation of a German pastor, with indications of permanence and usefulness. It was styled the "Fifth Presbyterian Church, German." From causes not necessary to specify here, the hopes that were formed of the success and usefulness of this enterprise, were not realized, and after a trial of about two years it was abandoned, the property sold, and the proceeds converted to other benevolent and religious uses.

Dr. Cunningham's pastorate closed as already stated, in May, 1860, and the church remained vacant until the following January, when Rev. J. Howard Nixon, of the Presbytery of Newcastle, responded to a Call addressed to him in the previous December, and entered upon his labors. Owing, however, to precarious health, he did not fully accept the Call until after three

months' service, and his installation took place on the
17th of April, 1861. As a very considerable number of
you enjoyed the privilege of sitting under his ministry,
it is not necessary to speak of it at length. You remember that his sermons were rich in evangelical
truth, sound and instructive in their bearing on christian
doctrine, in their practical relations always fresh and
appropriate, and the thoughts clothed in eloquent
and impressive language. God's truth as dispensed
from the lips of this able preacher did not return
unto him void. The average annual increase of membership during his pastorate, was greater than in
that of any former one; and as the population of
the city experienced a very rapid increase also during that period, it is almost certain the membership of
the church would have been still more enlarged, if
more sitting room had been available. It was common in those days to decline applications for sittings
because there were none to grant. This state of things
could not be allowed to continue. Accordingly, measures that had to some extent been discussed during
Dr. Cunningham's pastorate, looking to an enlarge-
ment of the building in front, were again brought up
and after full examination, with plans and estimates
were decided to be inexpedient. At a congregational
meeting held on the 16th of March, 1863, it was accordingly resolved to erect a new house of worship
upon the same site, enlarging it by purchase of two
lots adjoining on the north. The plan thus formed
was, perhaps providentially, delayed in the execution,

by the disturbed state of the community, growing out of the war, and by the rapid increase in the price of building material and labor. After the lapse of one year, it was thought practicable to commence active operations, and in the meantime it had become apparent that business was encroaching upon the "Circle," that the current of population was setting northward, and that the old site was no longer desirable for the same purposes. At a congregational meeting held on the 8th of March, 1864, the subject was fully discussed, the present site was recommended, and information given that it could be purchased for $22,500. The meeting approved the site, and ordered the purchase.

In the following year the church property was sold to the printing and publishing firm of Holloway, Douglass & Co., for $18,000, with reservation of the bell, pews and furniture, and the privilege of continuing occupancy until the first of April, 1866. On that day, being the Sabbath, Mr. Nixon preached a discourse embracing the history of the church from its organization to that time. The afternoon was devoted to a Sabbath School commemoration. Mr. James M. Ray presented a written narrative of that branch of the church work from the beginning; the School of the Third Church, with its teachers and officers uniting in the exercises. In the evening a re-union of this and the Third Church was held; the services were of an informal character, and several of the older members of churches of other denominations took part in them.

These were the last religious services in the old

church, and celebrated the exodus of the congregation from its walls, after an occupancy of twenty-three years. The work of demolition was begun on the following day, and in a very short time not one stone was left upon another, of what was, in its day, the largest and finest house of worship in the State.

In the meantime, the new chapel, or Lecture Room, had been begun and carried forward almost to completion. For two Sabbaths the congregation were like sheep without *a fold*, having no place of assemblage, but on April 22d, 1866,* that building was so far completed as to admit of occupancy, and on that day the congregation assembled within its walls for the first time, the Sabbath School, according to the original plan of the building, meeting in the second story. The corner-stone of the main edifice, was laid on July 23d of the same year, with appropriate ceremonies, in which the other Presbyterian pastors took part, and also several ministers of the Baptist, Methodist, and Lutheran denominations. From that time the builders' task was carried forward as rapidly as possible, and the sacred edifice was formally opened for public worship by a sermon from the pastor, on December 29th, 1867.* For financial reasons, the dedication was deferred until April 24th, 1870, when another pastor was occupying the pulpit; the dedication sermon being preached by Rev. Dr. Davidson, of Hamilton, Ohio.

The building committee to whom this enterprise

---

*This date was given incorrectly in the MANUAL of 1870, and also in that of 1874.

was entrusted were, Thomas H. Sharpe, Robert Brown-
ing, Jeremiah McLene, Addison L. Roache, William
Sheets, James W. Brown, John M. Lord, James M.
Ray, Thomas MacIntire and James Greene. Mr Thos.
V. Wadskeir, of Chicago, was the Architect, and the
whole cost of building and ground, $104,117.74.

While the erection of this noble house was in
progress, it was deemed expedient to establish a Sabbath School in a very needy locality, in the South-
eastern part of the city. Mr. William E. Craig, a member of the Session, took charge of the enterprise, and
so great was the success attending it, that very soon
the way was open for the organization of a church.
Mr. Calvin Fletcher and his associates in the ownership
of lots in that part of the town, presented two for the
site of a building; the estate of Dr. Coe presented
$500, and the congregation subscribed $2,800, for the
erection of it, and before our old house was vacated, a
neat, substantial frame church had been erected, and
which it has since been found necessary to enlarge.
The organization is now known as the Seventh Presbyterian Church, with a membership of 300, and a Sabbath school of 493, under the efficient pastoral charge
of Rev. Charles H. Raymond. When statistics were
gathered for our Semi-centennial Sabbath School cele-
bration in 1873, the school of the Seventh Church was
found to number 324 scholars, being much the largest
Presbyterian School in the city, and the largest but one
of any denomination.

The health of the pastor, Rev. Mr. Nixon, had be-

come so much impaired that soon after the completion
of this house, he asked leave of absence for six months
for the purpose of a sea-voyage, and a visit to Europe.
Consent was given, and the pastor left in February,
1868, the pulpit being ably filled in his absence, by
Rev. J. F. Dripps, a licentiate. Mr. Nixon returned
and resumed his duties on the 11th of October, but
without the full benefit to his health he had hoped to
derive from rest and travel. He toiled on however,
with the "thorn" of ill health rankling in his flesh,
until February, 1869, when he felt constrained to cease
pastoral work, and request a dissolution of the relation.
The church, with great regret, yielded to the necessity,
and the pastoral relation was dissolved on the 14th of
April, 1869, having been as already stated, the longest
of any in the history of this church, except that of
Dr. Gurley. It is gratifying to be able to state that
change of climate and several years' cessation for the
most part from ministerial work have wrought so great
an improvement in Dr. Nixon's health, (that degree
having been conferred upon him since leaving here,)
that he has recently taken the pastoral charge of the
Central Church, of Wilmington, Delaware.

During Dr. Nixon's ministry, in 1866, Messrs. Benjamin Harrison, Myron A. Stowell and William E.
Craig, were added to the Session; the last, a native of
Scotland, has returned, in impaired health, to his
native land.

Our next pastor, was Rev. Robert D. Harper, D. D.,
previously of the United Presbyterian Church, of

Xenia, Ohio. He was called on the 22d of April, 1869,
entered upon his labors here on the 16th of May, and
was installed on the 19th of October following; so that
the pulpit was vacant only about one month. Dr.
Harper's ministry is so recent, and so many of the present members of the congregation were among his ap-
preciative hearers and warm personal friends, that it is
not necessary to speak of it at length. It is sufficient
to say that he was sound and evangelical in his expositions of truth, warmly interested in his work, possessed
of many of the graces and charms of pulpit oratory,
and of marked courtesy and affability of demeanor.
Although no special revival occurred under his ministry
it was not barren of results, nor without the visible
seal of the divine favor. He tendered his resignation
on February 23d, 1871, after a ministry of less than
two years—the shortest thus far in the history of the
church—and accepted a Call to the North Broad
Street Church, of Philadelphia.

During Dr. Harper's pastorate, a corps of teachers
from this church assumed the care of a missionary field
in the North-east part of the city, where the Metho-
dists had planted a Sabbath School, which they called
the "Saw Mill Mission," but had abandoned it. Under
the diligent culture of that band of workers, and with
generous pecuniary aid afforded by one of the elders
of this church, the humble Missionary School has
grown into the Ninth Presbyterian Church, with a
membership of 131, and Sabbath School of 387, now
under the pastoral charge of Rev. L. Faye Walker—

being the fourth healthful and promising daughter of
this venerable mother.

During the same ministry, in the year 1870, the
congregation purchased this noble organ, not only as
an aid to the *songs of the sanctuary*, but also as their
grateful " Memorial" testimony to the favor of God be-
stowed upon the church at large in the re-union of the
branches known as the Old and the New School.

The vacancy left by Dr. Harper's withdrawal in
February, 1871, continued until June of the same year.
During that time, the Session was again enlarged by
the election of Messrs. James W. Brown, Jeremiah
McLene, Isaac C. Hays, L. B. Walker and Asahel D.
Benham. These brethren, together with Mr. Robert
Browning, who was elected to the same office in November previous, were ordained on the 9th of April,
1871, by Rev. L. G. Hay. Mr. Hays subsequently withdrew to the Memorial Church, and Messrs. Walker
and Benham have removed from the city.

Rev. Jeremiah P. E. Kumler, of Evansville, Indiana,
was called to the pastoral charge in June, 1871. He
accepted the Call, and entered upon his work on the
second Sabbath of July ; with the consent of the congregation, however, that he should carry out the ar-
rangements he had made for a summer vacation. He
returned and resumed his labors on the 12th of August,
and was formally installed on the first of October following. Although the time seems long since his departure, as it has been for the most part a period of
silent Sabbaths, it has not been long enough to efface

from your minds, remembrance of his earnest, devoted
ministry. He continued with us a few months less than
four years, but the results of that brief ministry are
not below the average of his predecessors. In the
proceedings had when the question of assent to his
withdrawal came up, the congregation resolved, that
the contemplated movement on his part was regarded
with regret and heart-felt sorrow; that he had en-
deared himself to the community as well as to the
church, as a christain teacher, adviser and friend, and
had, in a pre-eminent degree, illustrated the beauty,
the power, and the usefulness of an earnest and rugged christian character; that as a preacher of evangelical truth, he had proven himself not only rich in
Biblical learning, but fruitful in thought and suggestion,
and above all, most eloquently earnest. It is, therefore, not singular that the congregation declined assent
to Mr. Kumler's request for a dissolution of the pastoral relation, and took measures to have that dissent
most ably and eloquently advocated before the Presbytery. Mr. Kumler's convictions, however, pointed
in another direction, and the church finally, at a
subsequent meeting of the Presbytery, on the 14th
of September, 1875, signified their assent, perforce,
and the relation was dissolved accordingly. Mr.
Kumler accepted a Call from the Third Presbyterian
Church of Cincinnati, in which he is still laboring with
his accustomed zeal and energy.

A Committee of Supply, as usual, was appointed
after Mr. Kumler's withdrawal, to search out and re-

commend a pastor. Their first measure was to hear
Rev. James H. Brookes, D. D., of St. Louis, and the
result of their visit was, that in October, 1875, the congregation gave him a unanimous Call. Circumstances
in his own charge prevented him from giving a prompt
and decisive reply, but in December he visited us and
spent one week of active and appreciated labor,
preaching or conducting informal services every day
and evening, in this and other churches. After his
return home, the congregation voted a renewal of the
Call, which was subsequently enforced by visits from
some members of the Committee, and extended correspondence. But the result of the whole was that in
February of the present year, the Call was answered
with a final negative. Since that time the Committee
has diligently discharged its office, but with the sad-
dening result thus far of not finding a pastor acceptable to the entire congregation.

   What now remains to be said is chiefly in the way
of summary; and first of all, mention should be made
of the fact that this church, in its very early infancy,
adopted a plan of systematic contribution to the
Boards and benevolent operations of the church at
large. And though it is not pretended that it has,
through all the half century of its existence, done its
whole duty in that regard, or always given as the Lord
has prospered it, it may be truthfully asserted that it
has never lost sight of that duty, nor entirely failed in
the performance of it, despite the repeated "panics,"
the distractions wrought by war, and the oft recurring

"hard times" that have marked these decades. It would be interesting and doubtless encouraging to know just how much these contributions to the treasury of the Lord, through all these long years and manifold changes amount to. But unfortunately the requisite data have not been preserved.

In regard to the Sabbath School Institution, this church has an undisputed claim to the prime agency in its introduction into the infant community. Indeed before the church was organized, one of its founders and first elders, the only man in the settlement who had any practical acquaintance with Sabbath Schools and their management, had organized and was laboring in the old "Union School," which held its weekly gathering—not with the approval of all the settlers— in the immortal Cabinet Shop of "Squire" Scudder. This was the seed. The fruit we see to-day. And the ambition that is sanctified by God's spirit, can ask no more honorable memorial than that inscribed on the granite monument above Dr. Isaac Coe's remains in Crown Hill, THE FOUNDER OF INDIANAPOLIS SUNDAY SCHOOLS.

As an evidence of the harmony, as well as the efficiency with which the Sabbath School work in this church has been conducted, it may be mentioned that the office of Superintendent in it was for much more than half the fifty-three years of its existence, filled by one and the same person, Mr. James M. Ray. Others filling the office have been Benjamin Harrison, J. Albert

C

Vinnedge, Irving Harrison, Asahel M. Benham, Edward P. Howe, Elijah B. Martindale, William S. Armstrong and Ebenezer Sharpe.

In regard to ministerial service, you have seen that the church has enjoyed the labors of nine pastors and five Stated Supplies. Of the pastors, four are still laboring in other fields, and five have entered into rest. Of the Stated Supplies, but two survive. The eldership has embraced twenty-two members, all of whom except four, were ordained and set apart to the office in this church. Of these twenty-two, eight have crossed the flood; five have removed elsewhere; one has entered the ministry, and eight are now rendering service. The deaconship has always been recognized in the congregation as an important element of its working force, and is at this time filled by acceptable and efficient incumbents.

The entire membership of the church from the beginning, numbers 1,305, being an average of twenty-four per year, for the fifty-three years of the church's existence, and six for each quarterly communion: precisely what Dr. Nixon, in the historical discourse already referred to, stated as the average up to that time. Should not this failure of increase admonish us that while there remaineth very much land to the be possessed, the night cometh in which no man can work?

It is a more pleasant reflection that from the communion of this church, eight persons have entered the ministry. They are Rev. James S. Kemper, Rev. Henry T. Coe, Rev. J. Cooley Fletcher, Rev. L. G. Hay,

Rev. William W. Sickels, Rev. Edward C. Sickels, Rev. William A. Holliday and Rev. John Dixon.

It is a fact strikingly peculiar to the history of this congregation, that for the last twenty-five years, a considerable number of ministers of the gospel, not engaged in the work, have been connected with it. How far this has added to the moral strength of the church, is a question not now entered upon.

I have thus, brethren, perhaps with too much minuteness of detail, laid before you the history of this church from the day of its birth to this fifty-fourth year of its existence. To some of you it is the church of your fathers; to all of you, it is the church of your adoption and choice, and doubtless the object of your hearts' best and warmest affections. The time does not admit of an attempt to set out the lessons taught by this half century's history, nor is the speaker the person to adduce and enforce the duties growing out of the present juncture in your church affairs. Let me only remind you that the exigency which environs her, demands that all the true friends of the church rally to her aid. You are not satisfied that the sacrificial fire should be so seldom kindled upon this altar. You are not satisfied that so many Sabbaths should come and go, and no sound of prayer and praise and christian teaching, break the dismal silence within these walls. You deplore that this flock should be scattered simply because there is no shepherd to lead it in green pastures, and beside still waters. You can not believe that this church, much as it has done, has accomplished its full mission, or fully subserved the purpose of its Great Head. What then is the duty of the hour? Is it not that you manifest your sympathy with the Lord Jesus in the great purpose of his death, by increased activity in christian work, thus repairing as far as you may, the damage that results from a vacant pulpit? And seeing that God only waits for his people to attain a proper attitude before bestowing his blessing, what searchings of heart should there be, what fervent, constant prayer ascending from every household and every heart, until he return and repair these wastes of Zion, and pour down all the fullness of his blessing upon her!

And the blessing will come. God loves this church more than you can possibly do. He has graven her upon the palms of his hands : her walls are continually before him. Therefore, he will give her protracted life, and growth and prosperity. If not by our instrumentality, by that of others. Her coming half century will be more glorious than the first. In place of the fathers shall be the children, and when she celebrates her first centennial, and we are slumbering in the dust, and our names forgotten, doubtless she will have an experience to look back upon, of unmingled mercy, of enlarged usefulness and abundant blessing.

Record of Pastors and Stated Supplies.

Rev. David C. Proctor, Stated Supply, from October 1, 1822, to October 1, 1823; died January 17, 1865.

Rev. George Bush, Pastor, installed May 5, 1825, relation dissolved June 22, 1828; died in 1859.

Rev. John R. Moreland, P., called October 27, 1828, resigned May 15, 1832; died October 13, 1832.

Rev. William A. Holliday, S. S., served two years, from February 1833; died December 16, 1866.

Rev. James W. McKennan, P., installed June 16, 1835, resigned April, 1839; died July 19, 1861.

Rev. Samuel Fulton, S. S., served from January to April, 1840.

Rev. Phineas D. Gurley, P., installed December 15, 1840, resigned November 28, 1849; died September 30, 1868.

Rev. Charles S. Mills, S. S., served from November, 1849, to September, 1850.

Rev. John A. McClung, P., installed December 31, 1851, resigned September 29, 1855; died August 6, 1859.

Rev. Thomas M Cunningham, P., installed May 7, 1857, resigned May, 1860.

Rev. J. Howard Nixon, P., installed April 17, 1861, resigned April 14, 1869.

Rev J. F. Dripps, temporary supply from May to October, 1868, during pastor's absence in Europe.

Rev. Robert D. Harper, D.D., P., installed October 19, 1869, resigned February 23, 1871.

Rev. Jeremiah P. E. Kumler, P., installed October 1, 1871, resigned September 14 1875.

Rev. Myron W. Reed, P., installed October 4, 1877.

Record of Elders.

— ..

Isaac Coe, M. D., elected July 5, 1823, dismissed May 16, 1853; died July 30, 1855.

Caleb Scudder, elected July 5, 1823, dismissed September 23, 1859.

Ebenezer Sharpe, elected February 18, 1827, died August 1, 1835.

John Johnston, elected February 18, 1827, dismissed to Washington Church, Marion county, Indiana.

John G. Brown, elected February 18, 1827, died May 13, 1838.

James Blake, elected October 17, 1830, dismissed September 23, 1851.

James M. Ray, elected October 17, 1830.

Gov. Samuel Bigger, elected May 16, 1842, previously ordained to the office, dismissed to First Presbyterian Church of Fort Wayne, Indiana.

George S. Brandon, elected May 16, 1842, previously ordained to the office, died August 22, 1847.

Charles Axtell, elected February 27, 1850, previously ordained to the office, and subsequently to the ministry.

HORATIO C. NEWCOMB, elected February 27, 1850, dismissed September 23, 1851.

THOMAS H. SHARPE, elected February 27, 1850.

WILLIAM SHEETS, elected 1853, died March 4, 1872.

THOMAS MACINTIRE, elected 1853, previously ordained to the office.

BENJAMIN HARRISON, elected January 24, 1861.

MYRON H. STOWELL, elected October 11, 1866.

WILLIAM E. CRAIG, elected October 11, 1866, dismissed November 27, 1867.

ROBERT BROWNING, elected November 17, 1870.

JEREMIAH McLENE, elected March 7, 1871.

JAMES W. BROWN, elected March 7, 1871

ISAAC C. HAYES, elected March 7, 1871, dismissed September 1, 1874.

LEVERETT B. WALKER, elected March 30, 1871, removed from the city in 1871, dismissed January 7, 1878.

ASAHEL M. BENHAM, elected March 30, 1871, dismissed November 3, 1873.

MANUAL.

I. The standards of the Presbyterian Church consist of the Westminster Confession of Faith, and the Larger and Shorter Catechisms. To these all Church officers are required to subscribe, as containing the system of doctrine taught in the Holy Scriptures, and these are earnestly recommended to the thoughtful and prayerful study of all our members. But from the beginning of her history in this country, the Presbyterian Church has received to her Communion all those who, in the judgment of charity, were true believers in Jesus Christ, and who agreed to submit themselves peaceably to the rule of the Church, without requiring as a condition to Church membership the reception of *all* the doctrines taught in the standards of the Church.

II. CHURCH MEMBERSHIP.

The qualifications for membership in the Presbyterian Church are "knowledge and piety." There should be knowledge of the way of salvation, of the design of the ordinances of Baptism and the Lord's Supper, and of the obligations incurred by a public profession of the name of Christ. And there should also be a sincere reception of the Lord Jesus, as he is offered in the Gospel, and a full consecration of the heart and life to his service. It is the duty of all who believe in Christ to confess his name before men, by receiving Baptism, and by partaking of the Lord's Supper; and in this there should be no unnecessary delay, since the Apostle has taught us that with the heart man believeth unto righteousness, and with the mouth confession is made unto salvation.

Persons are admitted to the Church either by certificate from other Churches, or by examination by the Session.

III. RECEPTION OF MEMBERS.

[The candidates, standing in front of the pulpit, will be addressed by the pastor as follows:]

DEAR FRIENDS:—The Session having already received and enrolled you as members of this church, you do now publicly enter into covenant with us.

You have been deeply convinced of your personal sinfulness? You have heartily repented thereof? You have believed in the forgiving love of Jesus Christ? You here dedicate your heart and life to him? That dedication you are about to renew in the presence of God and this congregation?

You acknowledge God the Father, Son, and Holy Spirit—Creater, Redeemer and Sanctifier of men, to be your God?

You receive the Scriptures of the Old and New

Testaments as the word of God, and as the rule of your faith and life?

You believe that God so loved the world that he gave his Son to die for it ; that Christ appeared in the flesh ; that he set forth a perfect example of obedience ; the he purely taught the truth needful for our Salvation ; that he suffered in our stead, the just for the unjust ; that he died to atone for our sins, and to purify us therefrom ; and that he rose from the dead and ascended into heaven, where he ever liveth to make intercession for us? Therefore,

Renouncing all dependence upon your own works for salvation, you commit yourselves to Christ your Savior? Renouncing the dominion of this world, you consecrate yourselves to the service of Christ, your Lord?

You promise to remember his words, and to do his commandments by living a life of piety toward God, and of good-will toward men ?

You do covenant with this Church to observe its ordinances and to attend diligently its meetings for worship ; to submit to its rules and discipline ; to strive for its purity and peace, and to work together with us for the welfare of our fellowmen ?

WELCOME.

[The congregation standing.]

We, then, members of this Church, do gladly receive you. We welcome you to our communion, our fellowship and our work. We promise to love you, to pray for you, to watch over you, and by all means in our power to advance you in the Divine life.   Amen.

IV. CHURCH SERVICES.

1.   Religious services are held every Sabbath morning and evening, at the usual hours of public worship in this city.

2.   The Sacrament of the LORD'S SUPPER is administered on the first Sabbath of the months of March, June, September and December.

3.   The regular PRAYER MEETING is held on Thursday evening.

4.   The Sabbath School meets regularly every Sabbath afternoon, at half-past two o'clock.   Bible classes are also held at the same hour.   All the children and young people of the Church are expected to attend. Parents and others are cordially invited to be present, either as teachers, or as members of Bible classes.

5.   The Session meets regularly on the first Monday evening of each month, to receive applications for Church membership, either by letter or by examination.

OFFICERS.

Pastor.
REV. MYRON W. REED.

Ruling Elders.

JAS. M. RAY,   BENJAMIN HARRISON,
THOS. H. SHARPE,   JEREMIAH McLENE,
THOS. MACINTIRE,   ROB'T. BROWNING,
MYRON A. STOWELL,   JAS. W. BROWN.

Acting Deacons.

WM. J. JOHNSTON,   CARLOS DICKSON,
WM. S. ARMSTRONG,   CHAS. LATHAM,
CALEB C. BURGESS,   HIRAM J. CRAFT.

Trustees.

JAMES NICHOL,   W. W. JOHNSTON,
EBENEZER SHARPE,   JEROME B. ROOT,
                 JAMES W. BROWN.

Finance Committee.

R. S. McKEE,   EBENEZER SHARPE,
JAMES W. BROWN,   MERRICK E. VINTON,
                 W. H. H. MILLER.

Treasurer.
JAS. W. BROWN.

Clerk.
JAMES GREENE.

Superintendent of Sabbath School.
JAMES H. SMART.

Woman's Foreign Missionary Society.

The Woman's Foreign Missionary Society was organized in 1873. Its present Officers are:

Mrs. ANNE J. BURGESS, *President;*

Mrs. MARY E. SMART, *Vice President;*

Mrs. E. LOUISE REED, *Secretary;*

Miss GRETTA Y. HOLLIDAY, *Treasurer.*

It contributes to the Assembly's Board, through the Woman's Board of the North-west.

Its special object is the support of Mrs. LORETTA C. VAN HOOK, at Tabriz, Persia.

Its regular meetings are held on the last Thursday of each month. All ladies of the church and congregation are cordially invited to attend them.

There is also under its care, a MISSION BAND, composed of the children of the Church and Sabbath School, which meets in the afternoon of the last Saturday of each month.

ROLL OF MEMBERS.

In addition to the following ROLL, a *Reserved List* is kept, embracing the names of such members as have removed from the city without Letters of Dismission, or whose address has otherwise become lost.

ROLL.

Ankenny, Miss Sarah..........202 East Market.
Armstrong, Mrs. Keziah P...169 Ash.
Armstrong, Miss Ellie L......169 Ash.
Armstrong, William S.........28 Central Avenue.
Armstrong. Mrs Jennie.......28 Central Avenue.
Anderson, Miss Clara S........293 North Delaware.
Applegate, Mrs. Abby.........129 North Noble.

....

....

....

Beidenmeister, Mrs. Sarah...265 East New York.
Beidenmeister, Miss Mary J.265 East New York.
Belches, Miss Mary S. C......Fortville.
Benham, Henry L...............673 North Delaware.
Benham, Mrs. Mary S.........673 North Delaware.
Bobbs, Mrs. Catharine ....East End Georgia.

Braden, William..............Grand Hotel.
Braden, Mrs. Martha..........Grand Hotel.
Bradshaw, Mrs. Margaret.....264 North Tennessee.
Brown, James W...............97 West Vermont.
Brown, Mrs. Sallie M.........Room 1, Vajen's Block
Browning, Robert ....700 North Meridian.
Browning, Mrs. Margaret S..700 North Meridian.
Browning, Mrs. Mary..........South of City.
Boice, Augustin...............209 North Pennsylvania.
Boice, Mrs. Adele T. J........209 North Pennsylvania.
Barnes, Thomas F.............631 North Mississippi.
Barnes, Mrs. Elizabeth........631 North Mississippi.
Burt, William N..............824 East Washington.
Burt, Mrs. Maggie J..........824 East Washington.
Breckenridge, Joseph M......Lebanon
Burgess, Caleb C.............258 North Pennsylvania.
Burgess, Mrs. Anne J.........258 North Pennsylvania.
Burgess, Miss Anne Louise...258 North Pennsylvania.
Bryce, Mrs. Mary.............13 East South.
Bates, Ns. Doren.............352 North Alabama.
Bates, Mrs. Florence E........352 North Alabama.
Brink, Charles H.............151 North Illinois.
Brink, Mrs. Jessie............151 North Illinois.
Browder, Wilbur F............94 Hoyt Avenue.
Bacon, Hiram... ....Cor. Clifford & Keyst'ne Av.
Bacon, Mrs. Elizabeth.........Cor. Clifford & Keyst'ne Av.
Byers, Frederick....... ....
Byers, Mrs. Julia...............

Carlisle, John............Millersville.
Carlisle, Mrs. Margaret J.....Millersville.
Carlisle, Henry D ....
Carlisle, Mrs. Jennie A........
Carter, George.............544 North Tennessee.
Carter, Mrs. Mary Belle.......544 North Tennessee.
Clarke, Mrs. Rachel...........27 Lockerbie.
Cropsey, Mrs. Ann M........85 College Avenue.
Cropsey, James M.............85 College Avenue.
Cropsey, Miss Nebraska.......85 College Avenue.
Culbertson, Mrs. Mary E.....324 College Avenue.
Cruft, Miss Sarah R...........242 North Alabama.
Cummins, Miss Hattie H.....343 North Pennsylvania
Cassiday, Mrs. Mary F........326 North Meridian.
Craft, Hiram J...............827 North Alabama.
Craft, Mrs. Lou M............ 827 North Alabama.
Coffman, Mrs. Susie...........
Cox, Thomas...............269 Peru.
Cox, Mrs. Mary...............269 Peru.
Cox, Richard...............269 Peru.

Denning, Joseph N............98 North Mississippi.
Doughty, John G..............23½ Indiana Avenue.
Doughty, Mrs. Frances S......23½ Indiana Avenue.
D

Dickson, Carlos...............Grand Hotel.
Dickson, Mrs. Susan C........Grand Hotel.
Dixon, Hugh ....98 North Mississippi.
Davis, Mrs. Emma E...........North Tenn. North of 10th.
Downey, John T................130 North Alabama.
Downey, Mrs. Mary A........130 North Alabama.
Denny, Caleb S...............241 North Alabama.
Denny, Mrs. Carrie W........241 North Alabama.
Dollens, Robert W.............26 West New York.
Dollens, Mrs. Nettie............26 West New York.

Elliott, William J........... ...Cor. Tenth and Tennessee.
Elliott, Mrs. Charlotte........Cor. Tenth and Tennessee.
Espy, Mrs. Margaret E........930 North Tennessee.
Espy, Miss Kate E............706 North Illinois.
Elder, Mrs. Amelia E.........150 North New Jersey.
Elder, William B.............150 North New Jersey.
Elder, Miss Mary J............150 North New Jersey.
Evans, Miss Maria J...........Broad Ripple.
Egan, Mrs. Katie.............105 North New Jersey.
Eddy, Miss Mabel.............436 North East.

Foster, Chapin C.............762 North Pennsylvania.
Foster, Mrs. Harriet H.......762 North Pennsylvania.
Fitzhugh, Mrs. Anna.........417 College Avenue.
Fletcher, Albert E..........619 North Pennsylvania.
Fletcher, Mrs. Eliza S.......619 North Pennsylvania.
Foley, Mrs. Susanna.........North of Crown Hill Cem.
Foley, William W............North of Crown Hill Cem.
Foley, Miss Emma E.........North of Crown Hill Cem.
Fullenwider, John C.........308 College Avenue.
Fullenwider, Mrs. Mary E...308 College Avenue.
Fullenwider, Miss Lottie.....308 College Avenue.
Finch, Fabius M.............247 Park Avenue.
Finch, Mrs. Nancy A.........247 Park Avenue.
Finch, Miss Alice...........247 Park Avenue.

Gates, John J...............338 North New Jersey.
Greene, Mrs. Mary B........364 North Meridian.
Greene, Davies M...........364 North Meridian.
George, Henderson..........94 Harrison.
George, Mrs. Amanda........94 Harrison.
Gillespie, Mrs. Mary R......203 North Pennsylvania.
Gillespie, Miss May Ann.....D. and D. Institute.
Graham, J. Kearney.........180 North East.
Gibson, Reuben.............427 North Pennsylvania.
Gibson, Mrs. Nancy.........427 North Pennsylvania.
Gapen, Mrs. Martha.........569 North Delaware.
Goulding Mrs. Carrie........569 North Delaware.

Hammond, Upton J...........569 North Pennsylvania.
Hammond, Mrs. Lizzie M....569 North Pennsylvania.
Harbison, Alexander D.......146 Ash.
Harbison, Miss Agnes R......146 Ash.
Harper, John L.................328 College Avenue.
Harper, Miss Sarah E.........328 College Avenue.
Harrison, Alfred...............252 North Meridian.
Harrison Mrs. Lydia D.......252 North Meridian.
Harrison, Mrs. Bettie L. S...1038 North Illinois.
Harrison, Miss Mary S.........1038 North Illinois.
Harrison, Benjamin............674 North Delaware.
Harrison, Mrs. Carrie S.......674 North Delaware.
Harrison, Russell B...........674 North Delaware.
Harrison, Miss Mary S........674 North Delaware.
Howland, Charles A...........164 Parke Avenue.
Howland, Mrs. Helen.........164 Parke Avenue.
Howland, Charles B...........D. and D. Institute.
Henderson, Mrs. Rachel......710 North Meridian.
Henry, Miss Pamelia Alice...18 East Vermont.
Holliday, Mrs. Lucia S.......242 North Alabama.
Holliday, Miss Gretta Y......242 North Alabama.
Holliday, Francis T...........242 North Alabama.
Holliday, John H..............601 North Meridian.
Holliday, Mrs. Evaline M.....601 North Meridian.
Holloway, Mrs. Eliza..........277 North Delaware.
Howard, Mrs. Clarissa.........92 South Illinois.
Higgins, Charles J............Maine.
Higgins, Mrs. Sarah E.........Maine.
Humphrey, Samuel D.........
Hanna, Mrs. Rebecca A.......382 North Meridian.
Hanna, Mrs. Lizzie B.........382 North Meridian.
Houdyshell, John L...........D. and D. Institute.
Hawes, Mrs. Ada Augusta...476 North Tennessee.
Haynes, John R...............120 North Meridian.
Haynes, Mrs. Mary E. ....120 North Meridian.

Hussey, John R.................264 North Tennessee.
Hussey, Mrs. Mary J...........264 North Tennessee.
Hutchinson, Charles L........Pyle House.
Hamilton, Mrs. Emma.........Cor. Alabama and Sixth.
Houston, Miss Tina...........375 North Alabama.
Herr, Isaac.....................510 North New Jersey.
Herr, Mrs. Amelia..............510 North New Jersey.

....

....

....

....

....

....

....

....

Irving, Alexander B...........Hutchings Block.
Irving, Mrs. Mary..............Hutchings Block.
Irving, Miss Maggie Ellie.....Hutchings Block.
Irving, Cornelius L............92 West Seventh.
Irving, Mrs. Elizabeth C......92 West Seventh.
Irving, Miss Fannie Belle....92 West Seventh.

Johnston, Samuel A...........345 North Pennsylvania.
Johnston, Mrs. Estelle........345 North Pennsylvania.
Johnston, William J..........343 North Pennsylvania.
Johnston, Mrs. Fannie C......343 North Pennsylvania.
Johnston, Mrs. Mary..........699 North Meridian.
Johnson, Mrs. Mary ....474 North Pennsylvania.
Johnson, William P...........209 North Pennsylvania.
Jordan, Mrs. Mattie M........352 North Meridian.
Jones, Mrs. Flora C...........467 North Pennsylvania.
Jenks, George W..............Southwest of City.
Jenks, Mrs. Carrie E ....Southwest of City.
Jenks, Volney D...............49 Alvord.

....

....

....

....

Kirlin, James..................526 North Illinois.
Kirlin, Miss Mary J...........526 North Illinois.
Kirlin, Miss Sadie L..........526 North Illinois.
Kelley, Patrick H. .... 828 North Illinois.
King, Miss Martha J.. ....294 North Tennessee.
Kinser, Mrs. Nancy A.........Evansville.

....

....

Landis. Miss Gabriella.........504 North Delaware.
Latham, Wm. H...............614 East Washington.
Latham. Mrs. Lydia M........614 East Washington.
Latham, Charles...............614 East Washington.
Latham. Henry................614 East Washington.

Latham, Miss Lillie............614 East Washington.
Louden, Mrs. Lucy............130 West Ohio.
Louden, Miss Julia P.........130 West Ohio.
Long, Henry C................202 East Market.
Long, Mrs. Sarah C...........202 East Market.
Long, Mrs. Margaret..........202 East Market.
Lecklider, John T............327 East New York.
Lecklider, Mrs. Adelaide.....327 East New York.
Leonard, Mrs. Ellen T........North Indianapolis.
Lueders, Miss Catherine......484 North Mississippi.
Lueders, Miss Louisa.........484 North Mississippi.
Lueders, Miss Eliza..........484 North Mississippi.
Lueders, Miss Cornealia......484 North Mississippi.

....

....

....

....

Maguire, Douglass............78 East Ohio.
Maguire, Mrs. Anna G.........78 East Ohio.
Mitchell, James L............Grand Hotel.
Mitchell, Mrs. Clara G.......Grand Hotel.
MacIntire, Thomas............D. and D. Institute.
MacIntire, Mrs. Mary B.......D. and D. Institute.
MacIntire, Miss Martha L.....D. and D. Institute.
MacIntire, Miss Frances......D. and D. Institute.
Macauley, Mrs Anna N.........526 North Illinois.
Miller, Mrs. Elizabeth W.....Bates House.
Miller, William H. H.........185 Broadway.
Miller, Mrs. Gertude.........185 Broadway.
Martindale, Elijah B.........666 North Meridian.
Martindale, Mrs. Emma........666 North Meridian.

Martindale, Lynn B...........666 North Meridian.
Martindale, Charles...........666 North Meridian.
Martindale, Miss Susie.........666 North Meridian.
Mansur, Mrs. Jane............18 East Vermont.
Munson, Charles H............286 North Alabama.
Myers, Jesse D...............23 Chamber of Commerce.
Moritz, Miss Amelia C.........D. and D. Institute.
Morris, Austin W.............196 North California.
Merwin, Denton M............Rear 48 Yandes.
Merwin, Mrs. Lydia M.........Rear 48 Yandes.
McLene, Jeremiah.............139 North Pennsylvania.
McLene, Mrs. Mattie B........139 North Pennsylvania.
McDermott, Duncan...........Near Crown Hill Cemetery.
McDermott, Mrs. Mary........Near Crown Hill Cemetery.
McChesney, Mrs. Sarah J.....117 West Maryland.
McCheseney, Miss Mary J...117 West Maryland.
McGinnis, Frank..............
McKee, Robert S..............418 North Tennessee.
McKee, Mrs. Mary............418 North Tennessee.
McCoy, Hamilton.............390 North Delaware.
McCoy, Mrs. Ella B..........390 North Delaware.
McCommon, Patterson........Morgan County.
Mangun, George S ....Morgan County.
Mangun, Mrs. Cynthia J......Morgan County.
Milligan, Harry J............. 29 Christian Avenue.
Morgan, Mrs. Amanda........149 North Illinois.

Newell, Lyne S.................31 West Washington.
Newell, Miss Alice............383 Massachusetts Avenue.
Nichol, James M..............357 North Illinois.
Noel, Mrs. Elizabeth..........234 West New York.
Noel, Wood S.................387 North Illinois.
Newton, Mrs. Maria S.........99 Indiana Avenue.

....

....

....

Ogburn, Frank................23 East St. Joseph.
Ogburn, Mrs. Cornelia.........23 East St. Joseph.

....

....

Petrie William................297 Indiana Avenue.
Petrie, Mrs. Jane..............297 Indiana Avenue.
Purcell, Mrs. Atheline A......278 North Mississippi.
Porterfield, Henry C..........Bridgeport.
Parvin, Edward B.............580 North Mississippi.
Parvin, Mrs. Margaret........580 North Mississippi.
Pearson, Charles A...........141 North Mississippi.
Patterson, Mrs. Sarah J......511 North Illinois.
Potter, William H............10 Claypool Block.
Price, Miss Ida E.............D. and D. Institute.

Ray, James M...............166 East North.
Ray, Mrs Sophia P...........166 East North.
Ray, Charles A..............Washington, D. C.
Ray, Mrs. Laura A...........Washington, D. C.
Ray, Miss Florence..........Washington, D. C.
Roache, Mrs. Emily..........613 North Pennsylvania.
Root, Jerome B..............511 North Illinois.
Root, Mrs. Mary.............511 North Illinois.
Root. Miss Julia A..........431 North Meridian.
Rosengarten, Mrs. Mary......152 Broadway.
Rosengarten, Albert.........219 West New York.
Ross, Amos P................Citizens Bank Building.
Rorison, Brainard...........272 North Meridian.
Rorison, Mrs. Mary V........272 North Meridian.
Reed, Mrs. E. Louise........570 North Delaware.

....

....

....

....

....

....

Sharpe, Thomas H............239 North Pennsylvania.
Sharpe, Mrs. Elizabeth C....239 North Pennsylvania.
Sharpe, Miss Isabella M.....239 North Pennsylvania.
Sharpe. Miss Jessie.........239 North Pennsylvania.
Sharpe, William E...........239 North Pennsylvania
Sharpe, Ebenezer............621 North Pennsylvania.
Sharpe, Mrs. Frances A......621 North Pennsylvania.
Sheets. Mrs. Mary S. R......1038 North Illinois.
Sheets. Miss Mary R.........1038 North Illinois.

Sheets, Miss Anna H...........1038 North Illinois.
Sheets, Miss Katie R..........1038 North Illinois.
Sheets, Randolph..............1038 North Illinois.
Sheets, William H. H.........236 College Avenue.
Sheets, Mrs. Henrietta........236 College Avenue.
Sickels, Mrs. Alma C...........351 North East.
Sickels, Mrs. Sophia P.........351 North East.
Sickels, Henry C...............351 North East.
Sickels, Miss Alma C..........351 North East.
Skillen, Mrs. Margaret........48 North West.
Skillen, Miss Jennie A.........48 North West.
Skillen, Miss Nellie S.........48 North West.
Smith, Mrs. Minnie M..... ..Bates House.
Sponable, Mrs. Mary J........175 North Tennessee.
Stewart, Miss Margaret F.....226 North Meridian.
Stewart, Miss Mattie C........226 North Meridian.
Stowell, Myron A...............78 West Michigan.
Stowell, Mrs. Mary A..........78 West Michigan.
Swain, Mrs. Mary J..... ......41 North Illinois.
Swain, George H...............280 North Alabama.
Swain, Mrs. Sarah J...........280 North Alabama.
Smart, James H................258 North Pennsylvania
Smart, Mrs. Mary E...........258 North Pennsylvania.

Taylor, Miss Julia A............D. and D. Institute.
Thornton, Edwin C............Cor. Eleventh & College Av.
Terrell, Miss Emma............226 North Delaware.

....

....

Vinnedge, Joseph D...........California.
Vinnedge, Mrs. Kate..........California.
Vinton, Merrick, E...........748 North Meridian.
Vinton, Mrs. Susan V. M.....748 North Meridian.

....

....

....

....

Walpole. Mrs. Esther..........410 North Illinois.
Watson, Joseph S.............207 West Maryland.
Watson, Mrs. Sarah J.........207 West Maryland.
Wilson, Miss Sallie M........308 North Tennessee.
Wood, Alexander..............18 West Vermont.
Wood, Mrs. Sabina............18 West Vermont.
Wood, James D................18 West Vermont.
Woollen, Mrs. Mary E.........106 College Avenue.
Whiteside, Mrs. Mary K.......31 West Ohio.
Warne, Mrs. Albina...........430 North Tennessee.
Walker, Mrs. Margaret........126 North Pennsylvania.
Walker, Frank B..............126 North Pennsylvania.
Walker, John C...............126 North Pennsylvania.
Walker, J. F.................183 West Ohio.
Warren George S..............71 West Michigan.
Warren, Mrs. Harriet. ....71 West Michigan.

Williams, Lewis B..................144 North Illinois,
Williams Miss Mary L..........144 North Illinois.
Wiggins, Mrs Sarah H.........797 North Meridian.
White, Augustus B..............171 East Washington.

....

....

....

....

....

Youart. John M.................564 North Tennessee.
Youart. Mrs. Margaret R.....564 North Tennessee.

www.ingramcontent.com/pod-product-compliance
Lightning Source LLC
Chambersburg PA
CBHW021536270326
41930CB00008B/1278

* 9 7 8 3 3 3 7 2 9 2 9 9 7 *